Construction Zone

Rollers

by Rebecca Pettiford

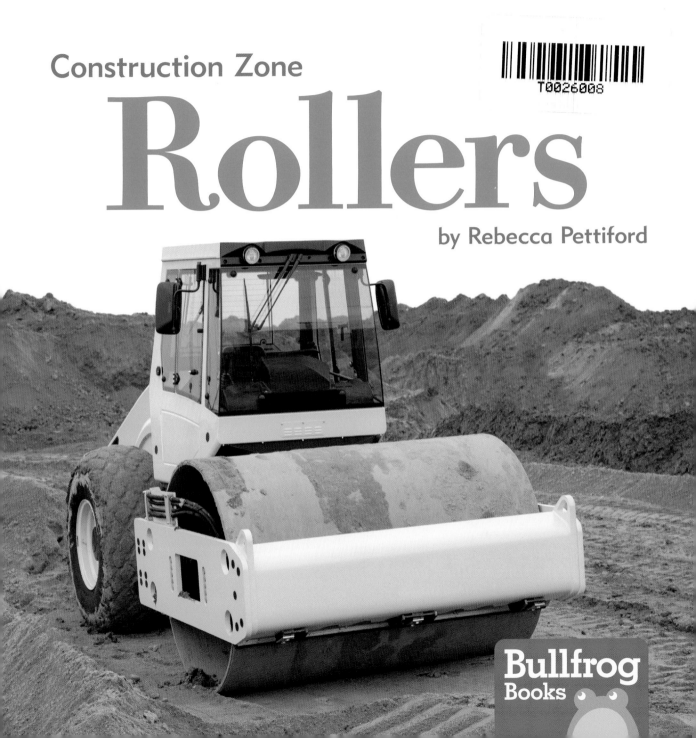

Bullfrog Books

Ideas for Parents and Teachers

Bullfrog Books let children practice reading informational text at the earliest reading levels. Repetition, familiar words, and photo labels support early readers.

Before Reading
- Discuss the cover photo. What does it tell them?
- Look at the picture glossary together. Read and discuss the words.

Read the Book
- "Walk" through the book and look at the photos. Let the child ask questions. Point out the photo labels.
- Read the book to the child, or have him or her read independently.

After Reading
- Prompt the child to think more. Ask: Rollers are big machines. They roll and compact. Can you name other big machines? What do they do?

Bullfrog Books are published by Jump!
5357 Penn Avenue South
Minneapolis, MN 55419
www.jumplibrary.com

Library of Congress Cataloging-in-Publication Data

Names: Pettiford, Rebecca, author.
Title: Rollers / by Rebecca Pettiford.
Description: Minneapolis, MN: Jump!, Inc., 2023.
Series: Construction zone | Includes index.
Audience: Ages 5–8.
Identifiers: LCCN 2021053820 (print)
LCCN 2021053821 (ebook)
ISBN 9781636908588 (hardcover)
ISBN 9781636908595 (paperback)
ISBN 9781636908601 (ebook)
Subjects: LCSH: Road roller—Juvenile literature.
Classification: LCC TE223 .P446 2023 (print)
LCC TE223 (ebook) | DDC 625.7—dc23/eng/20211209
LC record available at https://lccn.loc.gov/2021053820
LC ebook record available at https://lccn.loc.gov/2021053821

Editor: Jenna Gleisner
Designer: Michelle Sonnek
Content Consultant: Ryan Bauer

Photo Credits: Vereshchagin Dmitry/Shutterstock, cover, 3, 24; Maksim Safaniuk/Shutterstock, 1; Stangot/Dreamstime, 4; ewg3D/iStock, 5; SergeyZavalnyuk/iStock, 6–7; bogdanhoda/Shutterstock, 8, 23tl; fotosr/iStock, 9, 23br; Volodymyr_Shtun/Shutterstock, 10–11; Photoongraphy/Shutterstock, 12–13, 23tr; Terelyuk/Shutterstock, 14; Andrei Ksenzhuk/Shutterstock, 15; Andrew Ostry/Shutterstock, 16–17; ktsimage/iStock, 18–19, 23bl; dobrovizcki/iStock, 20–21; Konstantinos Moraitis/Dreamstime, 22.

Printed in the United States of America at Corporate Graphics in North Mankato, Minnesota.

Table of Contents

Roll and Press

A roller is a big machine.

It has a big drum.

drum

A roller drives.

The driver sits in the cab.

cab

New blacktop is laid.

blacktop

It is uneven.

The roller drives slowly.

The drum rolls.

It is heavy.

It presses down
on the blacktop.

It compacts it.

It makes a road!

More rollers help!
This one has eight wheels.

This one has two drums.

They all roll and press.

The bumps are gone!
The road is smooth.

Rollers do big jobs!

Parts of a Roller

What are the parts of a roller? Take a look!

cab

drum

wheel

Picture Glossary

blacktop
A hard black surface that covers roads and other paved areas.

compacts
Presses or crushes something to make it take up less space.

smooth
Having an even surface without bumps.

uneven
Not flat or smooth.

To Learn More

FACT SURFER

Finding more information is as easy as 1, 2, 3.

❶ Go to www.factsurfer.com

❷ Enter "rollers" into the search box.

❸ Choose your book to see a list of websites.